A Dime is a Sign

Poems of Love and Loss
(Feelings Into Words)

by Sherrill S. Cannon

Illustrations by Kalpart

Strategic Book Publishing and Rights Co.

Strategic Book Publishing and Rights Co., LLC
USA | Singapore
www.sbpra.com

For information about special discounts for bulk purchases, please contact
Strategic Book Publishing and Rights Co., LLC. Special Sales, at
bookorder@sbpra.net.

ISBN: 978-1-949483-20-8

Please also consider my award-winning children's books,
emphasizing consideration for others!
My Little Angel,
The Golden Rule,
Mice & Spiders & Webs . . . Oh My!,
My Fingerpaint Masterpiece,
Manner-Man,
Gimme-Jimmy,
The Magic Word,
Peter and the Whimper-Whineys,
Santa's Birthday Gift,
and
my first book of poetry, *A Penny for Your Thoughts*

Dedication

Special thank you to my daughters,

Cailin Rosemary Cannon Goncalves

Kerry Elisabeth Cannon Gallagher

my #1 Poetry Fans,

for their expertise and advice,

and for encouraging me to publish my poetry.

Acknowledgments

Special acknowledgement to my former mentor, Professor William Stahr of The American University, and a grateful thank you to Lynn Eddy and Robert Fletcher, who continue to make my books possible.

As in *A Penny for Your Thoughts*, this book is a compilation of poetry written through the years in an attempt to put feelings into words. As a former teacher, many of these poems were used to help counsel troubled teens and friends. I hope it will also be considered a book of healing.

A psychic medium once said that if you find a random dime, it is a sign that someone you have loved and lost is thinking of you.

A Dime is a Sign through Time

If you find a dime,
You will know that I'm
Sending thoughts of love
Through the veil of time.

Ten cents with a silver shine,
A sense sent you to help remind
That someone who left you behind
Is always living in your mind.

Sending love and vibes,
Felt as psychic sighs ...
The ones that you miss,
Send you a kiss ...

This collection of poetry contains many of these messages in poetic form.

THANK YOU

Thanks to the many people in my life –
students, family, and friends –
for allowing me to put feelings into words.
As a Valentine, I have always been preoccupied with love
in all its many forms, and I have also found great joy
in writing poetry. Please keep in mind that these poems are
empathetic and not autobiographical! *A Dime is a Sign* is a
companion to *A Penny for Your Thoughts* and combines
many more of my loves into a book full of feelings.

Special mention and many memories to:
Betsy, Bobby, Carol, Crystal, David, Debbee, Ellen, Francine,
Gez, Helen, Jesi, Jill, Joanie, Jody, Judy, Julian, Kate, Kim,
Laura, Livvy, Mark, Mike, Ted, Tina, Tori and many more.

And as always, thanks to my wonderful family:
KC, Christy, Kell, Steph, Kerry, John, Cailin, Paulo,
Megan, John, Josh, Parker, Colby, Lindsay, Tucker,
Kelsey, Mikaila, Kylie, Cristiano, Chloe,
my husband, Kim, and my brother Sandy.

Special thank you to KJ of Kalpart Illustrations
who has created the illustrations and book covers
for all of my books.

In loving memory of Michael Getler, mentor and friend.

Love & Loss: Coin Toss?

Table of Contents

HEADS . . . Of Love and Friendship

A Blessing

I hold you close ...
And from my heart
The angel wings of love
Enfold you and embrace –
Wrapping you in
Clouds of peace:
Powdery power ...
As God's blessing flows
From my heart
Into yours.

A Cascade

A tiny raindrop ...
A rivulet on a windowpane ...
A raging storm and tempest ...
Is my love.
A single droplet ...
A singing, babbling brook ...
A mighty, cascading waterfall ...
Is my love.
A primal spring ...
A rushing river ...
The endless ocean ...
Is my love.

A Code

Live, every minute of your life!
Never ever let a day go by
Without really feeling you're alive ...
You don't know when the time will come to die.
Experience all the relationships you can;
Do, all the things that you can do;
For there is no way you can know God's plan
Of how much future is allotted you.
Fill, all your days with happy times –
Make them into lasting memories;
So whenever happiness declines,
The past can give your future joy and peace ...
Never wait to show a friend you care,
For you don't know how long there is to share.

A Smile

The bright yellow sun
Looked down and gave me a smile:
Upside-down rainbow!

A Look

Never let that look go from your eyes ...
The one that stops my breath and grips my heart:
Electric current, surging as it flies
Between two poles of contact set apart.
In teeming mass of people, we're alone;
It shuts out all the world's reality:
That look that says "I love you" in a tone
Of powerful and rich intensity.
In midst of conversation, comes the charge
That deepens eyes with message it conveys;
And I can feel my soul and heart enlarge,
Receiving and transmitting love's deep gaze ...
And I can think and know of nothing else
But wonder, as on contact my heart melts.

A Song of Love

Try to hear the song that I am singing,
Harmonize with me within your heart;
Listen for the bells that now are ringing
Overtures of love that bid them start.
Drums are rolling with a silent thunder ...
Listen with your heart to hear my song;
Rhythms of a rare and gentle wonder
Echoing the theme of "I belong."
Cradled in your arms is my crescendo;
Singing lovely anthems high above;
Lulled to sleep in sweet diminuendo,
Humming tender strength, and warmth, and love ...
Promised peace and joy in soft refrain –
You, my source of melody, remain.

Contact

I take your hand ...
And let my love
Flow into you.
A touch
Means so much.

You take my heart ...
And hold it very
Close to you.
Your hug
Feels so snug.

CONVENTIONS

I'm too old to play games,
I don't care anymore –
I will give you a band aid
When I have a sore;
I will give you my gloves
When my hands are cold;
And if you are hurt,
Give you my hand to hold.
I will call on the phone
And not wait for my turn;
Whatever you're teaching,
I'll try to learn;
I will stop by to see you
And not mind the wait;
And tell you I love you
Before it's too late.
I will say that I'm sorry
When you have hurt me:
I will give you my love ...
Entirely free.

COVERS

I do not want to smother you –
I only want to cover you ...
To keep you safe and warm.
I'll draw the quilt up underneath
your chin,
Kiss you on the forehead,
Touch your cheek – a whisper on
your skin,
And blanket you with love ...
Then I'll tuck the covers more
snugly in –
And fondly wait for you to
kick them off again.

Cycles

If you believe in Love, believe in God:
Rejecting one, you do the other ban;
Repeating other pathways we have trod,
We'll go from god to God to Man to man.
We've passed from Spring to Summer, Fall, and Winter;
And gone from rain to sun to moon to stars –
So gradually our Hope's become a glimmer;
Away from Love, Apollo yields to Mars ...

Have you never felt the breathless moment
When a lover's look becomes a kiss;
And the surging waves of feeling's torrent
Wash and flood-transcend ecstatic bliss?
If with Love's deep gaze you have been awed ...
You have glimpsed the countenance of God.

Daughter of My Heart

Dancing in her eyes, the light of morning –
Eagerly awaiting each day's start;
Bright and sunny warmth, her soul adorning –
Beaming from the love within her heart.
In her inner self, a song of glory –
Expressing all the wonder that she sees;
Breaking from her lips, in joyous story –
Embracing life, to be what she must be ...
Notes of crystal shimmer in the sunlight –
Nightingale and lark soar high above –
Essence of the future's lovely star, bright ...
Radiant with faith and hope and love.

Deep Waters

Your hand reached out to touch my inmost heart –
It came to rest upon my tingling hair,
And all my senses concentrated there
At point of contact, while we sat apart.
Each strand became a nervous filament
Transmitted over synapse to the core;
As wave on wave of feeling reached the shore,
And surged forever in one brief instant.
Then to the hand, bow down the sensate cheek;
With gentle rub, caress – let gestures speak;
With petal cheek to tender hand bestow
The promise of the waters deep below ...
Torrential currents, under surface calm –
Revealed by ripples pressed upon your palm.

Dream

Last night I dreamed a quiet dream of you:
We sat together, letting thoughts be shared;
An honest time, with many feelings bared;
With contact, as with touch my courage grew –
And as I left, into your arms I flew.
You held me close – and so I finally dared
To say, "I love you," reveal how much I cared ...
You smiled at me and said you loved me too.
And then my heart was filled with joyous peace
That comforted and left my soul refreshed;
And all my tense anxiety was eased,
For with your love and friendship I was blessed.
When I awoke and found that all was true –
I spent the morning thanking God for you!

EMPATHY

You know the way I think, my Love,
You know the way I feel –
You put yourself into my mind
And feel the way I feel.
And with your deep-felt empathy,
You truly understand –
You reach out with your loving heart
And softly take my hand.
You warm me with your love, my Love,
As tenderly you kiss
Away the hurt and fears I have,
By knowing what it is
To love so deeply, love so much
That part of love is pain –
To know and feel and reassure
Again, and yet again.
And so I love you more, my Love,
With every passing day –
No matter what the future brings,
I'll trust, and hope ... and pray.

ENTRANCE

You came into my life with a flourish:

Glitter and fanfares – joyous hilarity,

Exuberant talent and glorious song!

And very, very quietly ...

You crept into my heart.

Eyes

Communication –
Expression of feelings,
Interpreted by eyes ...
That shine with the goodness
Of sharing more than words.

Happy and sparkling eyes,
Earnest and glowing eyes,
Accenting speech with meaning;
Saddened and misted eyes,
Loving and searching eyes,
Revealing the inner feeling.

Interpretation –
Of thoughts without speaking;
Communion of the eyes ...
That soften with the gladness
Of being overheard.

FANTASY

I'm happy when the time comes to put out the light –
For nighttime is the quiet time that I like best.
I put away my daytime cares and get undressed,
And snuggle down in bed for my nightly rite:
My thoughts become my eyes and give me sight –
I picture scenes, like greeting you as a guest
Whom you were not expecting – and before I rest,
I paint myself a fantasy of sheer delight:

I see you throw your arms out in welcoming embrace;
I hear your loving voice, feel the warmth in your eyes;
I sense your love for me and the smile upon your face
As you hold me close and hug me tight in glad surprise ...
All this I see and more, with my eyes shut tight
As I slip beneath the blanket of the long soft night.

FILMED MEMORY

I have a motion picture in my mind –
A memory forever in my head –
That captured such a very precious time
And all of what was done and what was said:
The way you sang your very special songs;
Bringing joy not just from what was sung,
But in the way you let yourself belong
Within the hearts and minds of everyone ...
For when you reached and touched, you became a part
Of every life that you helped to renew;
And you will always stay within the heart
Of every soul that shared that time with you ...
For very many films that day were made –
And many ones already there, replayed.

Hidden Sapling

I see my shadow lengthen on the ground,
As I grow taller with the passing years –
Showing me that all the fears that bound
Me to hide my leaves away unfound
By anyone – protecting me from jeers
Of scorn and laughter – had not been slowing
My growth. Now, I no longer fear rejection.
For during that time of hiding, I was growing
Up to meet the sun. And now I'm showing
All the leaves I have, since your affection
Brought me sunlight. Now, at last, I see
That what I have to give is not the shallow
And pale sprouts of yesterday; but deep
Rich and full leaves that have reality –
And must not be allowed to stay as shadow.

GODCHILD

Child of God,
So warm and full of light ...
Bringing beauty and love
To your world of people –
Making each one feel special ...
Singing your happy way
Through your joyous life ...

Longing for love,
Your love remains steadfast –
In spite of pain,
You seek to understand –
Opening yourself,
To help others unfold ...

Child of God,
So warm and full of light ...
You are my God-sign
That God is Love.

I LOVE YOU

I love you
The softness of a rose
With velvet blush;
Or the quiet hush
Of freshly fallen morning snows.

I love you.
My love like water falls
Around us
To surround us
With liquid-crystal magic walls.

My love,
You are the rose
That lives and grows
So deep inside me –
You are entwined with me,
Where you share my soul
And where you bring the sunlight
to winter snows.
You are my rose
That blooms and grows
So deep inside of me;

Where the waterfalls of love
Cascade within my soul,
Within my heart,
Within my soul,
You are a part

I love you.
My heart sings with your name.
Like sunshine,
You're my God-sign,
My lovely rainbow in the rain.

Your love brings the sunlight.
Your love makes my heart bright.
You are my soft rose,
You are love,
You're my faith
There's a God above.
Your love brings me rainbows,
Oceans where love flows,
Love flows,
Love grows.

I love you.
You are my life, my love;
My springtime,

And my sunshine,
My world and all of the stars up above.

I love you,
Forever, endlessly.
Like the ocean,
Love is open,
So deep and vast, and yet so free.

Oh, my love –
You will bloom in my heart for the
rest of my life.
I will love you forever, the rest of my life;
Forever, the rest of my life;
Forever, the rest of my life;
Forever, the rest of my life;
My love.

INSPIRATION

Do you know what you have done for me?
You have given me a chance to be myself;
Stimulated me to write a wealth
Of constantly inspired poetry.
You've given up your time to talk to me,
Restored my tired soul to greater health,
So I can write and think of nothing else
But ways to show my love in poetry.
You've inspired me to put my soul in rhyme,
Showed me how to live and still create ...
Given my heart a hug to show you care.
You've given me your friendship and your time,
Showed me how to love and still relate ...
Inspired me to write – and then to share.

I Would Give You…

I would give you the wind in the treetops,
The fragrance of flowers in June,
The moisture of spring in the dewdrops,
The pale shimmered light of the moon;
The soft, gentle rush of the river,
The faint melody of the lark ...
And the way that you made my soul quiver
As you led me up out of the dark.

Liberation

The stone on my heart is rolled away –
And all the dark and crawling things,
The guilty worms of suffering,
Are butterflies that greet the day.

The heavy weight of stone is gone,
The heart is light and starts to sing:
While gaily dancing in the spring,
The butterflies join in the song:

The song of love and trust and hope,
With happy thoughts on fragile wings
That flit and dart in spiraling rings
To form a gay kaleidoscope

Of whirling colors, shining bright!
The butterflies are fluttering –
They sense the joy of everything –
They feel the love that brings the light.

Love is Love

Love is love wherever you find it –
Man or woman, young or old –
A feeling of a special wonder ...
A heart to hug, a hand to hold.

Love is love, and if you find it –
Hold it very close to you –
Cherish it, for it is precious ...
Do not question why or who.

Love is love, and when you find it –
Open up your heart to share –
When you feel that special feeling ...
The spark between two hearts that care.

Love is love – whenever you find it,
Take it and never count the cost –
For what you find may last forever ...
But never found, forever lost.

Love's Spring

Within my heart I have a secret spring
That feeds the pool of feelings in my soul;
Where I can plunge, submerged – remembering
The source of love that keeps my spirit whole.

Sometimes when I am tired or depressed,
I dive into my pool and get away;
For in its living waters, I'm refreshed
By quiet peace at night and joy by day.

And sometimes as a lovely sweet surprise,
When I am doing other things, I find
An effervescent bubble will arise
To burst a happy thought into my mind.

Then late at night before I go to sleep,
I slip into my pool of deep emotion;
I swim in lovely memories I keep ...
And drown within the depths of my devotion.

My Garden

A garden is running rampant in my mind –
With all the flowers one could ever name,
And many weeds of every shape and kind;
All growing wildly, rank, and quite untamed.
It's going to take a lot of care to sort
The ones that should be helped to bloom and grow,
From the weeds that choke, and cut them short;
And then to place the plants so they will show.
For then, perhaps someday someone will find
A blossom whose great beauty will bring fame
And fortune to the one who was behind
The cultivation of the bloom that came ...
And I was hoping that it might be you,
Whom I could trust to show my garden to.

PRAYER

Defend, Oh Lord, this lovely child of Thine;
Endow her with the grace that You can give;
Bring her joy and laughter, love that shines
Over her as long as she may live.
Raise within her soul a song of songs –
Anthems of Your love, let her rejoice;
Happy in Your heart where she belongs –
Key to all Your love within her voice.
Bring to all who listen, thoughts of You
Ever singing through her to Your world –
Notes of sunshine and the rainbow's hues,
Nightingales, and roses soft and pearled ...
Enlightening all with beauty as she sings –
Revealing all the glory Your love brings.

My Strong Heart

Why do I love you? I cannot say –
My heart just feels – its only way –
And always seems to take control,
And loves with all its spirit and soul.

You seem to be the one it chose –
And when its love for you arose,
I had no choice, my mind was led –
I let my strong heart rule my head.

For you and I, we have no say –
It's going to happen anyway –
For what it feels, it's going to feel,
No matter whether right or real –

So we might as well accept its plan,
And go on doing what we can
To make things easy as can be –
And have a friendship, you and me!

PILGRIMAGE

My pilgrim ship at last has reached the shore –
Its time of searching finally at an end;
After seeking and peering around each unknown bend,
It has found the harbor that it was looking for:
An anchorage of trust, that has an open door –
Giving shelter for the sharing on which it can depend,
And a haven where its feelings no longer must pretend –
Yet a refuge where its love can continue to explore.

My ship had been sailing for such a long, long time –
Wending its way through the vast uncharted seas,
Sometimes losing hope that its port would ever appear.
Its sailors and talents had almost passed their prime ...
When in your sanctuary, they all received reprieves
As you gave your precious time – to listen and to hear.

Quiet Garden

The drowsy time before I sleep is best:

I seek the quiet garden in my mind

Where love and hope, like flowers intertwined

In fragile beauty, leave my heart refreshed.

My dreams in bright profusion sweetly dressed,

To make a garland of my thoughts, designed

To give me peace and joy; for I can find

The memories of you, like petals pressed.

So I in rosy thoughts draw close to you,

And meditate the wonder of a love

That yields such sweet bouquet of reverie;

Each dream a fragrant bloom of lovely hue,

Each thought a budding prayer to God above

To bless this garden path you walk with me.

RAINY DAY THOUGHT

Let the rain

In the skies

Combine with the

Sunshine love

In your heart

To give you a day of

Glorious rainbows!

REFLECTION

Eyes:

Reflect the soul within –

Hard, with dislike;

Cold, with reserve;

Masked, with indifference ...

Or soft and gentle with love.

When I look into your eyes,

Let me see your soul –

Soft, warm and open ...

To me.

Release

The anchor, heavy, encrusted,
Weighting me beneath the sea
Of cold currents – darkness –
Wavering in the sea-green murk,
Ever swaying – suffocating guilt and fear.

At last, the anchor rusted,
Broken chains of promises eroded;
Freedom – and an effervescent mind
Rising to the surface – bursting through
To taste the clear intoxicating air.

SERENDIPITY

Thank you for giving your time to me,
To give me peace and tranquility –
This sense of serendipity
That brings me such serenity.
For when you stopped to listen to me,
You helped my heart at last be free
To be the way it wants to be,
And see the things it needs to see –
Perceived with greater clarity.
And with this new ability –
And lovely calm quiescency –
Perhaps I'll find my destiny
In writing lasting poetry.

She Sings ...

She sings, and the world stops to listen –
There are smiles on all faces around;
For she shares all the love she's been given,
And gives all the joy she has found.

She sings, and a beauty surrounds her –
A light shining forth from her eyes;
As she gives to the people around her,
The love that the music implies.

She sings, and the world wants to hear her –
She sings, and all hearts sing along;
For the music she brings will endear her
Forever – for she is the song.

Sing for Me

Sing for me ...
Let me sit and listen with my being,
Absorbing into my self the glorious notes
Flowing with such sweet beauty,
Filling my soul with the melody of song ...
Sing for me ...
And let your heart fill up my heart
With the music of ourselves;
Capturing the beauty of the ages
In the rich melodious tones of your voice ...
Sing for me ...
And make my tears flow with the sound –
Lyrical splendor of the angels
Singing God and Love and Hope and Joy
In dulcet, mellifluous notes of gold and silver ...
Sing for me ...
Forever let me listen to you sing
The lovely gift that God has given you –
The only gift I ever ask of you:
Sing for me.

Special Garden

I must tend the garden of my mind –
The place where all the thoughts I'm thinking grow –
And hope someday, with care, that I may find
A bloom that to the world I'll want to show.
It has to be a blossom bright and new
That no one else has ever seen before –
Which, started as a seed, sprouted and grew
Into a plant of abundant metaphor
That symbolizes with its lovely flower,
The thoughts and feelings that are universal;
And places them inside a magic bower
Where they can find their roots within the personal –
For then my garden might cultivate and nourish
The hearts and minds of others to grow and flourish.

Special Moment

In your warm soft embrace, I feel
Secure and loved. I sense the quiet peace
Of really knowing that my love is real,
And not just dreams and fantasies.
Your gentle touch upon my hair enfolds
My heart within the magic of your caress.
I stand protected, close. The moment holds
All wonder and contentment. And I bless
The God that brought me to this special time
In my life – This lingering moment of utter joy,
When my world unites in lovely harmony. And I'm
Sure I never shall forget. I'll enjoy
It forever. I'll shut my eyes and remember your touch
And the time that I loved you so very, very much.

Special Place

From the depths of feeling in your heart –
Reaching out in music that you bring,
And your sunny joy in everything,
Naturalizing love in sounds of art –
Comes the spark that sets you far apart,
In the fertile place wherein you sing,
Nurturing talents with your inner Spring,
Enriching roots and helping new buds start.

How you give your music and your love,
And your warmth and light within your soul –
Nourishing lives, to gain a special place
Near the core, while lifting high above
All the lovely things that make one whole –
You and all you mean, we can't replace.

Springtime and You ...

Springtime and you came into my life together,

Bringing happiness and fresh beginnings too:

My heart was soft and sunny with the weather,

Basking in the light that came from you;

The birds within my soul began to sing,

Returning from the Winter they had fled;

And joy and hope and love began to spring

Within a mind that I had feared was dead.

The tiny seeds of talent began to grow

And blossom to your very gentle touch,

Refreshed by tears when eyes would overflow

Because I cared so very, very much ...

My arid self became a fertile place,

Tended by your beauty, love, and grace.

Sunshine

I turn my sun-starved face
To your warmth and light
And bask in the radiance
Of your love.

SPRING BIRTHDAY

A lifetime ago
You were born in the spring,
Bringing joy to my life:
You made my heart sing!
Each milestone you reached
Was a note in my song,
And the melody grew
As the days passed along.

Your beauty, your wisdom,
Your music and laughter
Accented the theme
And refrain that came after,
With love and great pride
And with gratitude too
For the harmony given
When God gave me you.

As you look toward your summer,

My song will be there

As a constant refrain

In a musical prayer

That the rest of your seasons

Allow you to sing

With the magical music

You brought me in spring.

Sunburn

When I see the love in your eyes,
I cannot look too long –
For like the sunlight, it burns
Into my soul and melts the inner me –
And I feel the warmth and light
Enveloping me –
Bringing a blush of feeling,
Like instant sunburn,
Spreading over me –
Revealing too much ...
So if I look away,
Or shut my eyes,
It only shows my sensitivity
To the intensity
Of love.
Look at me ...
Melt me.

Thank-You Note to God

Dear God,

Thank you for sending me this cherished person

Who has come to mean so very much to me.

So even though the time has come to leave –

Because the more I love, the more I grieve –

The copious tears I shed flow thankfully ...

For I have shared my heart, and let someone

Love,

Me

TALENT

The tiny seed lay dormant in the earth,
Feeling that its life span had run out.
It'd been so long since it had given birth
To even just a frail and fragile sprout.
It thought of all the fuss that had been made
When as a seedling, buds began to form
That showed the promise of a rare shade
Portending blossoms far beyond the norm ...
Too much attention caused the buds to curl,
To wither and withdraw without a bloom –
And then the passing time became a whirl
Of other growth that left the seed no room ...
Until the seed sensed love and space and light –
And rich profusion blossomed overnight.

THE BIRTHDAY POEM

When you were born, the angels sang

A song of joy and love –

For you were perfect and, to me,

A gift sent from above.

And as you grew, I stayed with you

And gave you all my time –

Each special moment formed a bond

That linked your heart with mine.

I heard the angels sing through you,

I saw them when you smiled –

I see them now as, all grown up,

You reach and teach a child.

I'm thankful for the angels' songs,

Our music without end –

For when God blessed my life with you,

He gave me my best friend.

THE CARESS

One day we talked of having an affair,

In bantering tone to hide the truth beneath;

And as you left, your fingers stroked my hair;

And I, because of trembling, could not speak.

You did not know you'd voiced what I had dreamed,

And that your touch to me was a caress;

You only thought you'd started what you'd schemed.

I wonder if you'd known or if you'd guessed

That toying with my heart would mean so much;

And once involved, would be forever so,

As guardian of my love and hope and trust;

That from a brief affair, a love would grow

Into the deep relationship we share;

I wonder ... would you still have touched my hair?

THE CRUCIBLE

Into the crucible

Of leaden burdens

And molten dread,

Came a refining fire ...

Melting a will of iron

With the carbon

Of shared feelings

And confidence –

Fused into a new love ...

Of shining tempered steel.

THE DAM

Still and deep, the waters massed behind
The wall that passing time had caused to form,
To stop the flow of words within my mind ...
Collecting force with every passing storm.
The pressure grew with every drop of pain
Absorbed into my saturated soul;
Until my heart no longer could contain
The flood of feelings, spread beyond control
To form an ocean many fathoms deep –
With currents running swift and strong below.
And then you came – and love began to seep
Beneath the wall, and then to overflow ...
In a torrent of words I pray will never cease –
Bursting from my heart, in glad release.

The Kiss in Your Eyes

Eyes darken

And become opaque,

Intensified and deeper –

And I feel myself drowning

In the depths of feeling ...

Melting, dissolving,

Merging and fusing –

Sinking into the oblivion

Where consciousness ceases

And breathing stops;

In the rarefied atmosphere ...

Quiet, intense,

Surging and charged –

The electrified vacuum

Where, eyes locked –

Time stops ...

In love.

TREES

Trees, straight and tall, reaching toward the sky,
Lift up their heads to look into the sun,
Bend with the wind when it is passing by,
Fold their leaves in prayer, when the day is done.
Drinking in the rain, helping life to grow ...
Cleaning up the air, releasing oxygen ...
Clenching tight the earth, reaching deep below ...
Linking earth and sky in unity again.

Trees give us beauty within their symmetry –
Sheltering and shading, or standing bare and free –
Trees provide a home for birds and squirrels and bees –
Fruits, nuts, and wood are gifts of God through trees.
Trees give me peace and free me from all strife,
By joining man and God, and symbolizing life.

THE TREE

Today my singing heart beheld a tree
In green relief against a summer sky:
A strong and solid arm uplifted high
With open palm, a leafy canopy.
Umbilical cords to earth, its roots to me;
As if appendage, bound with earthly ties,
Still with its verdant fingers had to try
To touch the ether-blue eternity.

Yet, pointing toward the sun – its deity;
Deprived of fertile soil, it would die:
Thus, human hearts must strive to upward fly;
Yet, nurtured by a love's fertility.
Today I saw someone I deeply love ...
And heart engendered thoughts that flew above.

THE SPARROW AND THE EAGLE

The deepest vanity I have
Is hoping you might care;
That maybe if I give my love,
You just might want to share.
What false conceit has prompted me
To think I merit you?
What value could you place upon
What I can say and do?

Why should you care for what I give?
You are better than I –
What can the tiny sparrow do
To help the eagle fly?
Admiring his majesty,
Aware of powered wings,
The mighty eagle soars aloft;
The sparrow only sings.

And yet I offer loving songs
To let you know I care;
Hoping, in your mighty flight,
That you will be aware
That what I have to offer you
Is loyalty and love,
No matter if you're on the ground
Or soaring high above.

And if you want me for a friend,
My songs will never cease;
For knowing that you love me too
Will give me greatest peace;
For I could know within my heart
That love need never die ...
And that the sparrow's loyal songs
Might help the eagle fly.

VALENTINE

I am your Love

And you are mine

And so together

Our hearts combine

To be forever

One valentine,

For I am your Love

And you are mine!

Visions

Come to me, my love, and let me see
All the glorious wonders your love brings:
Lovely soft roses with petals of gossamer wings –
Pearled with dewdrops in a panoply
Of rainbows, shimmering in sunlight ecstasy –
Blooming in a heart where music sings
The strong, deep vitality of eternal Spring ...
That when you bring your love, you give to me.

Water cascading, with magic crystal walls –
Creating a world of pristine crystalline prisms,
Transforming myriad raindrops into waterfalls ...
Boundless water, surging in gentle rhythms,
Swelling with the rocking of the sea ...
This, when you give your love, you bring to me.

WE ARE ALONE

When I walk into a room,
And you are there ...
You are the only one in the room.
Worldliness vanishes –
No one is there –
We are alone.

We talk –
Of mundane things
And ethereal things ...
Of everything.
And then ...

When I look into your eyes,
And love is there ...
I find eternity in your eyes.
Consciousness vanishes –
My heart stops –
We are, alone.

WORSHIP

I love you with my heart and soul and mind,
And deify your goodness and your grace:
For you to me are gentle and divine,
And I see God reflected in your face.
You are my master, Lord of heart's domain;
The ruler of my soul – omnipotent;
And I will ever glorify your name,
And praise you with a love magnificent.
For you have given me a chance to see
A miracle created to attest
That God is love – by sending you to me:
A vision of His love made manifest ...
For all the parts of me were unified,
In you – my god – in love, personified.

Your Hand

I take your hand, and send my love to you ...
Giving, with my touch, my inmost heart.
Can you feel the current flowing through
The point of contact – joining every part
Of me to you? Does it stop your breath
As it does mine? Can you feel the surge
Of love that spreads throughout – the depth and breadth
Of it – the bonding, as our feelings merge –
Electrifying? And when I hold your hand
And grip it tightly, letting feelings flow
Into your heart – do you understand
That this is how I let emotions show?
I drop my head down to your hand and pray ...
Thanking God for blessing me this way.

Your Name

My eyes caress the sight of your face
My mind responds to your brain
My ears tune in to the sound of your voice
And my heart sings the sound of your name.

It whispers with longing, it shouts with great joy
Repeating it endlessly o'er
I smile with your unspoken name on my lips
And the sound of it deep in my core

It sounds of my tenderness, tells of my love
The wonder and joy that I feel
The sound of your name is the song in my heart
Making daydreams and memories real

It keeps you within me, a part of my self
The song of your name in my heart
And I'll sing that sweet song for the rest of my life
For you're part of me, even apart.

SPINNING—Of Related Emotions

A Poem

You sent me a poem
(I think it was you)
Describing a moment
That I never knew ...

A tentative feeling
Of love in the air
Portrayed with an image
Of quiet despair

As the portentous moment
Revealing love's joys
Was disrupted by sounds
Of a motorbike's noise ...

And the now broken moment
Reduced to a page
Of unrevealed passion
That never could age ...

A Child's Eye View

I can remember life when eye-level was the sink,
And I had to ask for help – even for a drink:
When people towered tall, their faces up so high
That I had to look up to them – way up to the sky.
When they said to jump, I jumped without a blink;
And it didn't matter very much, what people think.
So if I hurt myself, I went ahead and cried,
Expecting love to comfort me and make me satisfied.

So why is it so hard, now that I'm grown up,
To look up to or depend on higher authority ...
And why am I afraid to go ahead and jump,
Because of what is thought by those observing me ...
Why can't I cry when my love feels so unsure ...
Oh life is so much harder, now that I'm mature.

After the Packers Have Left…

I sit quietly in my house
With boxes piled everywhere –
Nothing's where it's supposed to be,
And everything's disrupted.
All is quiet …
And strange.
And I ponder on a life
With pockets of love everywhere –
But nothing's where it used to be,
And friendship's interrupted.
All is quiet …
And changed.

Appreciation

I have known you but a third of a year –
A time made more precious because I knew
Ahead of time that soon the time would disappear
And I would have to leave. And so all through
Our limited time together, there was a sense
Of urgency – to pack into that preset time
As many experiences as possible – to condense
A lifetime into a few months. And I'm
So glad I had that predetermined span –
For even though I wish that I could stay,
At least I know that I have done all I can
To value every minute of every day
That I could spend with you. And I know
I'll have many memories with me when I go.

Acknowledgement

Your heart cries out in silent pain
For what is happening;
Your plea is bitterness, to deny the pain
Of love and loyalty betrayed.

And my heart answers in empathy
And identification with your heart,
Knowing the confusion from deep searching
For answers that are superficial and inadequate.

To know that love IS,
And always will BE,
But only for the one who LOVES;

And the thought that the one who is loved
Does not love
According to one's belief in love,
Cannot be accepted.

And I want to take your pain
Into myself; to keep your love alive
By entreating faith and courage to believe;
And in so doing, strengthen my own belief.

And suddenly I must acknowledge
That which I have always known yet fought;
Feelings hidden, unbidden, and thus must remain
Until, if ever, our hearts are allowed to commune.

For in that small moment
Of feelings so deep,
Of sharing love's pain ...
I find love again.

A Quest

There's a longing in my heart,
That nothing seems to help appease ...
A constant searching for a feeling,
That its inner core perceives
But never touches, only brushes
In its own reality;
As it searches for contentment,
Reaches for security.

All the love that it is sure of,
All the friendship it achieves –
Never gives true satisfaction,
Only hints, which taunt and tease ...
I must find that feeling somewhere –
Someone who can give to me
The kind of love I'm always seeking ...
To clasp my heart, and set me free.

A Star...

Just as a star glitters and sparkles and dazzles
In beaming its shining bars into the void,
Looking for contact to make itself real ...
Lost in the brilliance, your heart looks for love.

A Spark

From a spark, a flame has started burning
Softly in my heart – warming me
To feel once more the longing and the yearning
For a love I sense may come to be ...
A little spark – started long ago
But left to smolder on its own, while I
Went off to tend an ember still aglow
Within the heart of someone else. To try
To keep a fire going, giving hope
And love, fueled with my heart and soul.
That fire's blazing strongly, yet the smoke
Is all that's left to me. And now my whole
Self is grateful for that hardy spark ...
That bright new flame that keeps me from the dark.

Before

Before I met you,
My life was full –
I was happy
And content ...
But now
I know
What I
Missed.

DISTRACTION

Take my hand, so I can concentrate
On what you're saying, instead of thinking that
I wish that we could touch. I hate
To think of other things, while we chat
Of things that mean so much – All I need
Is contact ... To lean my head against your arm
And feel you next to me, so I can heed
The signals that are coming through – to warm
My heart and set me free to think of what
You're telling me. Because I love you so,
I need to send my love by touch – but
I also want to hear what you want me to know.
So take my hand and let's communicate ...
Let us touch, so I can concentrate.

FIRE

My little flame is slowly dying out ...
The feelings that ignited it have blown
Too hard, too fast to let it grow. I doubt
That it can burn much longer on its own.
I should have blown more gently – given time
For it to catch – Let you add some fuel
To it, so it could grow stronger. But I'm
Afraid that I was too intense. Now you'll
Have to be the one to tend the flame –
To see if you still wish to share a fire
Of warmth and love, where two hearts feel the same –
And work together to make the flames grow higher
Until they burn with sure intensity ...
While I give to you, and you give to me.

Forever

Forever is a time of no goodbyes.
Remember this, even if my eyes are wet
And no matter if my poor heart cries:
Never will my inner self forget
Caring for you – feeling my love grow
Inside me, till it filled my empty space ...
Never from me will you really go –
Ever in my core, you have your place.
How could I forget? For you're inside ...
Always in my self. So, though I grieve –
Notice that I do not say goodbye,
Now that it is time for me to leave ...
As I know our ties will never sever –
You will be within my heart forever.

It Doesn't Matter

It doesn't matter whether you love me –
What matters to me is that I love you –
That I keep that love within my heart,
And keep on feeling the way I do.

It's not important that you love me –
You have your busy life to live –
Just go on letting my feelings start ...
I'll understand, and I'll forgive.

For I don't care if you have love –
I know I have enough for two –
It stays inside me when we're apart,
And is always there to share with you.

So, don't respond, just take my love –
I have so very much to give –
For of my heart, you have a part ...
And with my love, you help me live.

Giving

I gave you a present and got satisfaction
From knowing the gladness it gave in itself;
And by giving a tangible symbol of love,
In giving to you – also gave to myself.

I gave myself pleasure by making you happy,
I cherished the chance to give something to you;
For I gave you a keepsake reminder of me,
For I was the giver – and knew that you knew.

Acknowledged bestowal rewards in itself;
Benevolent feelings are giving's attraction;
In giving, receiving – without sacrifice,
I made myself happy by my benefaction.

But then I found out what true giving can be:
I gave you a gift without letting you know;
I loved you enough to give up what I wanted,
Without making sure that you knew it was so.

It cost me much more than mere money alone,

But I got so much more than just money can buy;

For I found I could give out of sheer love for you,

Not letting you know that I gave as a tie.

Unlauded bestowal rewards to the soul;

Unselfish giving yields deep satisfaction;

In true sacrifice of myself for your good ...

For your happiness, was my benefaction.

LEAVES FALL

The leaves are waving goodbye –
Falling to earth in royal tones
Of crimson and gold –
Obeisance to autumn:
Confetti for the procession
Heralding majestic winter,
Promising the return of the monarch
And the spring coronation.

LONGING

Take my heart
Wrap it in love
Squeeze my hand
And make everything all right.

Touch my soul
Feel what I feel
Ease my pain
And hold me through the night.

IF YOU CARE AT ALL ...

If you care at all, please

let me know

By giving up your time to

talk to me.

If you care at all, please

tell me so

And let my heart respond

in poetry.

If you do not care, please

don't pretend –

Even though my joy will

not go on –

For falseness causes pain, and

in the end

I'll be much more alone, with

what has gone.

So, if you care at all, please

share with me

Your honest feelings, deep

inside of you.

And if you do not care, please
let me see –
Even though it breaks my
heart in two –
For then I can at least
maintain my pride,
And put my opened heart
back inside.

Moving

My life seems to have become a series of
Goodbyes. I move from place to place, finding
New friends whom I can trust – to give my love.
And I can't really stop myself from minding
When I have to leave again. It seems
A shame that each new start has to end
Before it has a chance to mature. My dreams
Of permanence, when finding a close friend,
Are over before they really have begun.
But I have found that when I go away,
The point at which I leave is a good one:
For the love that has been started seems to stay ...
And deep inside, my heart really knows
That my life is also a series of new hellos.

Merger

I hear your voice ...
And spinning back in time,
Reach for the ageless inner core
of love –
Superimposing maturity on youth ...
Speaking with my heart to your heart:
To the girl in the woman,
The woman in the girl transposed ...
Changing lives –
Changeless love ...

My Advice

They're only small for such a little while,
And soon, no longer crawl into your lap
To get a hug or kiss or loving smile ...
They give up their dependence, like their nap.

As they grow older, they become real friends –
It means so much to share with them their lives,
To help them reach their goals, achieve their ends,
And finally see them grown, with husbands, wives ...

That it is really not a sacrifice
To give that extra time, for each demand.
One's inner talents can be put aside,
Till they no longer need to take your hand ...

But never let that spark within you die –
And save a special time for your husband too;
So when your children leave, you'll stay alive
Within the love that he still shares with you.

Needs

You need space to look around you –
I need love to let me see;
I need crowding, close connection –
You need distance to feel free.
You need time to be alone in –
I need having time to share;
I need constant deep communion –
You need visits short and spare.
You need room to move about in –
I need being next to you;
I need love the way I need it –
You need love the way you do!

Night Sounds

The wind breathes through the leafy treetops,
Bringing sounds of the surf and the sea ...
Surging crests, velvet nighttime raindrops,
Whispering sounds of the ocean to me –
I slip away in the rocking deep ...
And close my eyes ... and drift to sleep.

ONLY I KNOW

You can never know what you mean to me,
Because you do it unknowingly ...
Only I know.
The sound of your voice when you talk to me,
The tenderness and the sincerity ...
Only I know.
The depth in your eyes when you look at me,
The compassion and the love I see ...
Only I know.
The touch of your hand when you comfort me,
The goodness and the security ...
Only I know.
The feeling of peace when you listen to me,
So freely and understandingly ...
Only I know.
The friendship that you have given me,
So quietly – so thoughtfully ...
Only I know.
The pain I will bear when you part from me,
So hopefully – so helplessly ...
Only I know.
The knowledge that love will continue to be,
Forever – for always – eternally ...
Only God knows.

PLEASE WRITE

One difficulty with loving someone who
Makes little effort to contact me, is that
There is really nothing I can do –
If I am the only one who makes contact –
To guarantee a relationship that will last
When times and places and circumstances change.
For without the links connecting what has past
To the future, the familiar may become strange;
And what has meant so much, will start to fade
Into a hazy memory – not quite real –
A silhouette of shadow in the shade.
To keep the sunshine in the way we feel –
The contact that has meant so very much –
You must try to help me keep in touch.

PERHAPS...

I came to you, upset and scared –
Reluctant to confide ...
For if I put it into words,
It couldn't be denied.

You filled my heart with so much love
There wasn't room for fear –
And brought a light to chase away
The shadows drawing near.

You stayed beside me, held my hand –
Gave me strength to bear –
And at the time the verdict came,
You were there to share.

You smiled and cheered and held me tight –
We laughed until we cried –
And now that I'm alone again ...
Perhaps I should have died.

Predecessor

If I get to heaven,
I will wait for you –
I wouldn't want to be up there
Unless you're coming too.
I won't mind the waiting –
Enjoy your life each day –
I'll be watching over you
And join you when you pray.
And when your life is over,
I'll meet you cheerfully ...
For I will never enter heaven
Until you are with me.

Presumption

I thought that you were looking forward, too,
To sharing such a special time with me –
How very vain and foolish, now I feel,
To think you'd want to share my poetry.

How could I have presumed so very much
Upon your interest; had nerve to ask for time;
Or considered that someone as talented as you
Would care to share my very silly rhyme.

For in my heart, I dared to feel you care –
And I still want to share my verse with you –
I should not have thought, presumed, or dared ...
And yet I did, and I could've, and I do.

QUANDARY

"Find another friend" –
It's easy to say ...
But how do I tell my heart
To feel that way?

How do I tell my heart,
"Love that one instead" –
When love comes from the heart,
Not from the head.

And how can I tell my heart
To love or to feel?
For only when it's felt,
Is a feeling real ...

And how can I force my heart
To feel or to love –
When love is a special gift
Of God above.

How can I make my heart
Feel that special spark –
When all around, it finds
No light – just dark?

And how do I stop my heart
From feeling so much –
From wanting to give to you –
To share, to touch –

And how can I make my heart
Look for someone new?
No matter what I tell it,
It still loves you.

QUESTIONNAIRE

Will this chance ever come to me
Again – or is this the only chance I'll ever
Have to do it? Will the opportunity
Pass me by – so later I will never
Be able to repeat it? Is the time
And effort all worthwhile – so I can make
A memory to last forever in my mind?
These are the questions I ask myself, for the sake
Of determining importance and priority –
To help me find out what's best for me to do.
For after I check to see if the majority
Of answers are affirmative and true ...
I cast my logical answers into the blue,
And do whatever my heart tells me to!

QUESTIONS

Questions – unanswered –
Whirl in my mind:
Pipe dreams? Real promise?
Wasting my time?

Shall I continue?
Give it all up?
Is there a future?
Is present enough?

Where are the answers?
Who will give help?
How can I find out?
All by myself?

Why am I trying?
What should I care?
There are no answers ...
Not anywhere.

PRETENSE

They say that "close" we should not be;
To you I'm nothing ... just a "friend."
But our hearts know that could not be;
We go on loving ... and pretend.

REACH OUT ...

Reach out to me – I think I need a hug

To warm my heart. Just a gentle touch

To show me that you care – so I feel snug

And safe and loved. It means so very much

To have you be the one who reaches out ...

For I am still unsure – afraid to let

My feelings show. The coldness of my doubt

And insecurity freezes me. And yet

I long to be the one to reach out to you ...

Let your sunshine thaw my reserve. For I

Need the contact and the comfort too ...

To warm my heart and encourage me to try.

So please reach out – give me a hug, and then

I promise I will give it back again.

REGRESSION

You hold me close, and I curl up inside
And I become a little child again ...
Feelings that adulthood has denied,
Respond when you let your heart open
To hug me – allow me to regress – become
Dependent on your strength and warmth and love –
And I am still a baby with my thumb
In mouth – not sure of what I'm afraid of,
But grateful for the comfort – being held
Close and stroked, calmed and supported
By love. The tender feelings that are felt
Within the heart should never be aborted –
For there's a baby in each one of us ...
That remembers hearing heartbeats as a fetus.

See-Saw

See-saw –

I see ...

I saw.

The present, bright,

Was gone at night.

My love today,

Passed away.

The truth, revealed –

My love, repealed.

What seemed so right –

Perceived insight ...

See-saw –

Eyes, see ...

Heart, saw.

SELF-CONDEMNATION

Hypocrite! Damn you to the ends of your false world!
Strip away the blind self-righteousness from your mind;
Tear down the wall of martyrdom around your heart;
Wake up and see yourself for what you truly are:
A selfish, immature, thoughtless mediocrity.

You have practiced the ultimate in hypocrisy:
You profess selfless love and deep understanding;
And then turn around and show your utter lack of it,
By being selfish enough to cause renewed pain,
Just because you feel that you need to be understood.

You have had the audacity to deem yourself good:
You deify your ideal of unselfish love,
In your world of "loving without need to be loved";
Preaching feelings that you can't honestly feel yourself.
Hypocrite! Damn you to the ends of your false world!

SHELTER

My love, I need to be with you tonight ...
To feel your arms around me, close and warm,
Enfolding me in softness, holding tight –
Protecting me in safety from the storm
Within my heart – The raging winds that cry
Their tears of loneliness and aching pain,
Tearing through my soul, laden by
The drenching streams of never-ceasing rain
Falling from my heart. In my despair
I need the shelter of your arms to still
The tempest of my thwarted needs – to share
The deep contentment and the quiet thrill ...
Oh, hold me close and let your sunshine start
Forming lovely rainbows in my heart.

Space

I know you have a secret private place
Inside of you – a little hidden recess where
You keep your special thoughts and feelings. There,
Within that inner core, is love. A trace
Is all you show from time to time – in case
Someone might get too close and want to share
That sheltered spot inside – might make you care
Too much – might threaten to invade your space.
How can I make you see that love does not
Demand more than it gives – to help you know
That loving is a strength – to understand
That if you let yourself be loved a lot,
You'll still be free? Allow your love to grow –
Be truly free – Reach out and take my hand.

Success

Inexorable crawl –
Ragged fingernails on
bloodied, splintered
future artifact –
Relentless grueling infinitesimal
caterpillar tread
Over indefatigable corpses –
Manhood's subliminal woe –
Struggling to reach the pinnacle
in excess of quintessential
double standard ...
Kudos, Ms. President!

SPAN OF TIME

I offered to her a bridge – constructed
By years of thought and enlightenment,
And light-years of experience;
Transcending; to understanding and constancy,
And the boundless ability to love more than one,
Without taking away from another; unchanging
Yet regenerating.

How can I expect her to cross my bridge
Woven of cobwebs – solidified
By the slow passage of many years?
Have I forgotten my once-held resolution
Never to love again; or my inability
To fathom the superficial proposition
Of loving more than one?

I cannot build her bridge, nor offer mine

To span the years of doubt and anguish

Of bitterness and refusal to feel;

Even to ease pain or quicken understanding.

She must build her own bridge for herself – in her own time;

For my bridge of steel – incomprehensible – to her

Is only gossamer.

Suspension

If I put it
Into words,
It will be
Real ...

So, I hold it
In my head –
And only
Feel ...

TELL ME

Tell me that you love me, let me see
The love within your eyes; let me hear
The tone within your voice that says to me
"You are special, you are very dear,
And you are Love." Hold me in the warm
And tender touch of eyes and voice – and say
The things I need to know to help me form
My life. So, as I go along my way
Without you by my side, but in my heart;
I'll know that you would really rather be
With me, sharing all we have – a part
Of each other's lives so totally ...
And if you feel your longings shouldn't show –
Tell me with your eyes and voice – I'll know.

TELL ME A STORY

Tell me there is no God! ... and then insist

That early people thought up in their heads

A lovely tale – The Bible – which is myth ...

(Is your name Lazarus? Were you dead?) ...

And how there is no Heaven and no Hell,

No after-life, nor knowing those we knew;

Just worms that eat us, and decaying cells ...

(Did worms, then, try to eat you too?) ...

And when you speak of "miracle" of birth:

Tell me of eggs and sperm, that people earth;

And how the primal life came from the sea,

Evolved, transformed, and Man did come to Be ...

First: Tell me there is no God. (And then explain –

Whence came first drop of life within the main?)

THE END

I think I've lost the will to write –
The poems are still within my head;
But without someone to share them with,
I'd rather go to sleep instead.

How can my life have changed so much?
Before, I could not go to sleep,
For all I cared to do was write –
To get them on a page to keep.

I wonder if I've wasted time?
I thought perhaps there were a few –
That might have made it all worthwhile ...
I hoped to share them all with you.

But now it seems you do not care ...
I think I'll let this be the end –
My inspiration's gone somewhere ...
My mind went back to sleep again.

THE PARTY

See the two – the ones so much in love
That even in a crowd, they're still alone ...
So conscious of each other all the time.
He will not let her stray far from his side,
But hovers near, embracing with his eyes;
She must feel warm and deeply satisfied ...
She stands within the circle of his care –
That aureole of light they seem to share,
Encircling each with overlapping light
Making all it touches seem more bright;
So if someone would stand between the two,
The glow would shed a light upon him too ...
And see the way they constantly must touch –
The way that as they move about, they brush
Each other with their hands and fingertips,
In subtle contact, as with touch a kiss;
As if to reassure that each is there,
And each of each is constantly aware ...
He brings her glass, and lingers with his hand
Upon her hand, in loving gesture – and
Removing it, they pause remembering;
The pressure of the contact lingering ...
And when he lights her cigarette, he lifts

His hand, in hers, as offering a gift

Which she brings softly forward to her lips,

And sensuously inhales with silent kiss;

Then gently flowing back, relinquishing

The contact of his hand, still everything ...

And see how they commune with darkened eyes

To speak of love, that now between them flies

And streaking over synapse to the core,

Enfolds the heart in silence, saying more ...

They stand apart, yet in awareness one –

As if, in passing, they could feel the sun

Upon the two, their shadows intertwined ...

They stand together, obvious –

And to the world around, oblivious ...

And who would guess – to see their happiness –

That what they have together, can't be blessed?

For each of them is to another bound –

And they must lose what they, together, found.

THE DAY THAT MARY DIED

The day that Mary died was bleak and gray,
For tears of all the world were being shed –
The mournful sun had turned his face away:
The mother of the Son of God was dead.
The mourners gathered round to pray and cry –
They wept for all the sorrow she had known:
She'd borne a child for God, then watched Him die
Upon a cross, forsaken – mocked – alone...
A few remembered hearing angels sing
That though He gave His life, He rose again –
They wondered if for Mary, death would bring
The life her son had promised would begin ...
And in the crowd, the face of Jesus smiled,
For on his lap was Mary, infant child.

THE TELEPHONE

I sit and will the silent phone to ring;
Hoping that your mind has been on me,
Answering the thoughts that toward you wing,
Responding to my love's telepathy.

Every time it rings I hope it's you.
Running to the phone, I say a prayer
That somehow you have caught the thoughts that flew,
And when I pause to listen, you'll be there.

And so I am enslaved by telephone,
Waiting in its silence for its sound;
Instant flares of hope whenever it rings.
Sending flying thoughts, I wait alone;
Close within its call, my heart is bound –
Yearning for the joy that your voice brings.

THE UNANSWERABLE

How can I let you know that I love you,
And make you know that you do not have to love me?
How do I tell you that for me it is enough to love?
Feelings can't be controlled – either to feel or
to not feel,
And so I cannot force myself to stop loving, anymore
then you can force yourself to start.
Or must I explain?
And how do I explain the unexplainable?

How can I keep from telling you I love you;
And not make you feel obligated to feel in some way?
How shall I keep my eyes from saying what my heart
feels,
And myself from revealing an eagerness to be near?
(Could it be that perhaps you already understand
and have not misinterpreted?)
Yet could I prevent?
And how do I prevent the unpreventable?

How can I temper my intensity of feeling,
Yet remain at peace with myself in my heart?
How can I reconcile my desire to ease your pain
With the overwhelming urge to comfort you in my arms,
And not force you to reject me; and in the destruction
of my dreams, to destroy me?
So should I avoid?
And how do I avoid the unavoidable?

How can I make you admit that you might care,
Without causing you to feel disloyal to another?
How may I beg you to keep your mind open to love;
Without asking for love, and dual recognition of it?
Could it be that I am only fooling myself – and that
there is really nothing there?
And could I accept?
And how do I accept the unacceptable?

TRUST

You can't take love, for you're afraid to love –
To really let your mind and body go;
To let someone share all you're dreaming of,
The hopes and fears you want no one to know.
You want to keep your feelings set apart,
Protected by an independent wall
That sometimes lets a person touch your heart,
But never lets one person hold it all.
And yet there's so much love inside of you –
An untapped fund of feelings trapped within;
That if you trusted – let your love grow too –
Could be a way to let your life begin
To have new meaning. You'd have love so deep
That you could look for someone else to keep.

VERDICT

I spread my self before you –
My inner soul I bared ...
My guilt revealed, I closed my eyes
And wondered why I'd dared.

And suddenly my shadows
Were suffused with wondrous light ...
You held me close and whispered
That it really was all right.

VESPERS

Give to me your very special love –
Even though the future's far away,
Near to me please let your sweet heart stay
Ever giving hope and love – I pray
Vespers for the morn I'm dreaming of.

In my heart I long to be with you ...
Embracing you with all the love I bear,
Vowing that someday, our lives we'll share,
Enfolding you forever with my prayer
Enveloping all we think or say or do,

Bringing comfort and security
Bound within the knowledge that we keep
Ever in our hearts. Although we sleep ...
Remembering the promises so deep ...
Till the bright day dawns when you're with me.

Vulnerable

If I open my petals to you,

You must be very gentle

With your touch ...

For my inner core

Will be open to you,

And I will have

No defenses.

So, if I must be pruned,

Give me time

To close up just a little ...

And then I will

Open to you again,

And grow.

Who Me?

You think you know me –
But the me that you know,
Is only the person
I am with you – so
The me that I am
With somebody else,
Is not the me you know –
With you, I'm myself!

WALLS WITHIN

Love – the foundation of emotion,
Building walls – within;
Of bitterness and frustration,
Of pain and anguish,
Of resentment and anger;
Of refusal to care ...
But not indifference.

Love – the prerequisite of living,
Building walls – within;
Of forgiveness and understanding,
Of loyalty and steadfastness,
Of constancy and devotion;
Of refusal to hate ...
But not insensitivity.

Love – the epitome of feeling,
Building walls – within;
Of determined preservation,
Or resolute destruction;
Of continuance or cessation;
Of martyred feeling ...
But not insensibility.

Wall of Apprehension

A nice thing happened to me today –
But I was afraid to call
To share this thing with you,
For fear it'd mean nothing at all

Except to be a bother,
And impose on the time you are free,
And make you stop what you're doing
To have to listen to me.

How can I care for you,
The way my heart decrees –
When I am afraid to call
To tell you of something that pleased?

What is wrong with my heart,
To feel the way it feels –
When I seem to bother you,
As I fear your voice might reveal?

I only know I love you,
And so, I will dare to call ...
And I hope you will care enough
To help me tear down my wall.

When I'm with You...

When I'm with you, my heart is sure –
I feel protected, loved and safe –
I have direction, I feel secure –
The ties that bind me never chafe.

And yet whenever you're not here,
And I'm alone, I come apart –
My nameless longings reappear,
And I have such a restless heart –

For nothing seems to satisfy –
I wander through my lonely life,
In search of ways to pacify
My discontent and inner strife –

For I need you to make me whole –
When you are gone, I am unsure –
I need your ties to bind my soul ...
I guess I'm still just immature.

You, Friendship — I Love

I see you now – just sitting there alone,
And thinking thoughts with no one there to share;
Knowing that, if mentioned, I would care –
But wary, lest by contact, love condone.
And so you cannot write, nor even phone
To keep alive the friendship that is there;
Lest by your gesture, find to your despair
That once again, my love you must bemoan.
Oh, would it not be better to accept
The friendship and the love I offer you –
Without still asking what I cannot give?
The love without the friendship, both reject;
But Friendship without Love cannot be true,
For like the two of us, can't fully live.

Your Place

There's a place in my heart that is empty:

The place that belongs to you.

And the place will remain

Till you come back again,

For nobody else will do.

There's a time in my life that is vacant:

The hours that you used to fill.

And the time will remain

Till you come back again;

Until then, they'll be hours to kill.

There's a part of myself that is missing:

The space that you left behind.

And the void will remain

Till you come back again,

Only then will I be whole in mind.

TAILS . . . of Heartache and Anguish

ALTHOUGH I LEAVE YOU...

My heart is weeping, way deep inside –
It shows in tears I cannot hide,
Because I'm leaving, to go away ...
Please tell your heart, my love will stay.

And through the years when I'm not there,
Please don't forget, please stay aware ...
And know I love you – I always will –
Although I leave you, I love you still.

My heart is crying, although I know
That in my soul I'll never go –
For when I leave you, my love will stay
Through all the time that I'm away.

So, through the years when I'm not there,
Please don't forget, please stay aware ...
You know I love you – I always will –
Although I leave you, I love you still.

Please don't forget me – I'll always care –
And if you doubt, just say a prayer –
My love forever with you will stay ...
And I'll be with you, each time you pray.

All through the years when I'm not there,
Please don't forget – just say a prayer
To know I love you, and always will –
For though I leave you, I love you still.

I'll not forget you, though we must part –
For part of me is in your heart.
I'll dream my daydreams of you each day,
And keep my memories of yesterday.

All through the years when I'm not there,
I'll not forget, I'll stay aware ...
Because I love you – I always will –
Although I leave you, I love you still.

ANGRY RAIN

Angry rain

Lashing at my window pane

Searching for entry

Making water webs on screens

Surf-sounding wind-driven splashes

On my transparent barrier – Screams

Of pain.

BUCKET LIST

I have a lot of things to do
Before my life is done:
I put them in a great big sack
And do them one by one.

But as my sack grows lighter,
Almost an empty sack ...
When did my great big bulging sack
Become just a small stack?

CHANGE

I will love you forever –
That cannot be changed ...
In one shared experience
My life rearranged –
For love was established
And life was reborn,
As sunshine comes after
A violent storm.
You gave me a rainbow,
I gave you my heart –
I thought that my loving
Would cause yours to start.
Now I find more clouds massing,
The barometer dropping;
For my pressured intensity
Shows no signs of stopping.
I cannot stop loving you –
But I'll show how I care ...
By veering away from you,
And clearing the air.

CHERISH

Cherish is a word
As the song implies,
For the feeling in your heart
That makes you realize
That what you feel is deep
And strong and true ...
A love within your heart
That comforts you

Cherish is a song
That lives within my head,
Reminding me you're gone
But can't be dead ...
For I will cherish you
With love we share,
And keep your love alive
Within, by prayer ...

Conclusion

We had a time of love and ecstasy,
A chance to let our hearts merge into one;
A time of love to live in memory ...
We started what we knew should not be done.

It never would have worked, it could not be;
The obstacles too great to overcome:
You were too young, and I could not be free ...
We ended what should never have begun.

DELUSION

Let it go – It's over anyway.
For though you reach, you cannot touch
A shadow that's begun to slip away.
It was delusion, that meant so very much –
A fantasy – an imaginary dream –
Something that was never really there.
It had no substance – was not what it seemed:
For as you grasped, it dispersed into the air.
You had an illusion of something that was unreal,
A fleeting glimpse of something you couldn't see;
But as you reached, you could sense and feel –
Before it faded into unreality –
The unattainable form of love's ideal:
The elusiveness of love's security.

DEMAND

Misguided Masters:

Comprising authority, compelling conformity;

Concealing hypocrisy, commending democracy;

Conveying amenity, constructing nonentity;

Connoting morality, confounding reality;

Containing audacity, commanding what has to be ...

Look what you've done!

You've:

Conceived enmity, and corroded beauty;

Confused loyalty, and corrupted duty.

What else can you do?

Can you:

Control sensitivity?

Consume creativity?

Disciplined Despots ...

Leave us alone!

Flower Show

I'm the prettiest rose in the garden –
Surely, they'll notice me,
For I'm taller than the others –
I know that they must see.

I know that I have beauty;
My scents and hues agree –
I should have won already ...
Oh, why won't one pick me?

EVOLUTION

Another year has rolled around the sun
As time turns into seasons one by one,
And what has been the future now has passed
While we discover all that seems to last ...
The love that once so passionate has gone,
Evolving into friendship's lingering bond ...
And we no longer speak, although we talk –
Our steps no longer running, slowed to walk.
We find that love keeps changing day by day,
And miss the love we've lost along the way ...
But love the effervescence that has sprung
Into our hearts, where we're forever young!

EXHORTATION

Dear baby daughter,

Grow to be pretty

And graceful and loving;

Know how to cook and clean,

And raise children;

And to be smiling and giving,

And to listen ... and serve ...

But do not try to think,

Or to feel,

Or to beat your head against that

Terrible wall that will not let you

Be a mind

But a body.

Echoes

I hear the haunting voice that calls,
Echoing off invisible walls,
Yearning for what cannot be:
The day that you belong to me ...

The softly sighing whispered breath
That comes before the gasp of death
Reminds me of what cannot be:
While only night belongs to me.

Flash

Tiny spark ...

Kindled flame ...

Burning flare ...

Blazing fire ...

Excess fuel ...

Searing flash ...

Smothered embers ...

Wisp of smoke ...

Total dark.

Focus

When I was young I hoped to find
A love on which I could depend
To stimulate my heart and mind:
A future love without an end.

God granted what is His to give:
A love that made my spirit whole;
And in my present, let me live
To love with all my heart and soul.

But now I find I'm looking back
To find what once I thought would last –
There's something my life seems to lack:
I live in memories of the past.

I Cannot Write

I am sad
And all alone –
My mind is dead,
My heart is stone.
I cannot write
Nor see nor phone
The one who from
My life has flown,
And left me waiting
On my own,
Without a loving
Touch or tone –
I miss the tender
Love I've known –
I'm empty, lost
And all alone ...
(And this is such
A lousy poem.)

LAPSE

You woke my mind:
And once again I feel ...
I want to think,
To share,
To love.
But now –
Awake and feeling –
You choose body over mind ...
And I think
I want
To go back
To sleep.

Meant to Be

Some memories are best unremembered;
Forgotten and tucked far away
From thinking of dreams that have shattered
And turned all my rainbows to gray ...

There seems to be method in madness,
And many things are meant to be;
But some of them result in sadness ...
And that is what happened to me.

MISLED

I'm not going to die ...

Why should I?

Instead –

I'm going into exile ...

For a while.

I dread

Not seeing you again ...

Who knows when?

Ahead –

We may find at the end,

My dear friend ...

I'm dead.

Parting

"I miss you, I miss you,"
Loneliness cries –
"I'm with you, I'm with you,"
Remembrance replies.
"Not all ways, not all ways,"
Resentment defies –
"For always, for always,"
Steadfastness supplies.
"I'm lonely, I'm lonely,"
Bereavement still sighs –
"If only ... if only ... "
Contentment denies.

MY PROBLEM

You see ...

I love you.

I wish you loved me.

For then, perhaps

I could be free

Of all the longing

And the anxiety

That tears at my heart,

And will never let me be

Completely

Happy.

For, you see,

I love you ...

I wish you loved me.

PLEA

I am a mind,

Trapped alive:

Thirty-six, twenty-four, thirty-five

Under one hundred thirty-three.

No one sees me ...

Just my shell.

Please listen ...

And tell.

Premature Goodbye

Wait! You weren't supposed to go before
I had the chance to say goodbye to you!
You said we'd get together and explore
The ways we could revive our love anew ...

But now you've gone – and I am so alone ...
My heart remembers what has been before,
And every night I listen for the phone
That never rings ... I realize nevermore ...

REVELATION

Could it be I did not know the meaning,
And the deeper depths you touched in me?
Realizing now, with aching feeling;
Opening my eyes, at last I see ...
Love, when did you creep into my heart?

Silently I watch and see you leaving,
In my heart I cry out to you, "Stay";
Still you must not know that I am grieving,
Calling for you not to go away ...
Just when did you creep into my heart?

REMINDERS

I see your face in my mind's eye
Whenever I stop to dream awhile:
Your image appears – I see again
Your eyes alight with that special smile ...
If memory dims, I only have
To look at a favorite photograph.

I hear your voice in my mind's ear
Whenever I pause to reminisce:
I hear the music and the songs
And relive all the times I miss ...
And if memory fades, I can escape
By listening to a favorite tape.

But what can I do to relive the sense
Of feeling you hold me close to you?
There is no way – just emptiness
And nothing I can really do ...
For I have nothing that captures your touch
And the feeling of closeness that means so much.

Song to Myself

Memory of singing heart's fulfillment –
A way to sate my thirst or only whet?
Remember you can only bring him ruin –
If you keep away, could you forget?
Transcend yourself and relish what he gave you;
Avow your love by sacrificing ties;
Long for him forever, and still savor
Love, the taste of which unveiled your eyes:
Only know that he must never love you ...
Repletion that you long for is denied.

Sorrow

I am a house with an underground stream
That courses deep beneath my foundation,
And pulses underneath; yet never seems
To give me any cause for trepidation.
Currents, strong and full, are there – but I
Have solid walls protecting me; so when
The storms drench all the earth, I still am dry
And safe from feeling anything ever again.
The stream beneath me is my only flaw –
Yet my heart is hard; my walls set me apart.
In my Winter, I'm not aware at all ...
Yet if in Spring there is a sudden thaw,
The flooding feeling rises to my heart –
Composure cracks, and tears seep under my wall.

THE PRICE

Where are they now? The gifted souls and minds
Of creativity – The genius ones
That now could help the world with special finds,
Discoveries – New ways to new dimensions:
The music that the world will never hear,
The sciences and arts now lost to men,
The leaders that we need – they can't appear,
For seeds that are destroyed can't grow again.
For in those generations wiped away,
Who knows what greatness was forever lost –
What brighter world we might have had today,
If we had not allowed that horror – and cost
Of lives and talent. We must forever pay
With sorrow for all we lost in the Holocaust.

This is It

This is it. This is really it.
There are no tomorrows planned. The time
For us to say goodbye has come. It hit
Me this morning, when I awoke, that I'm
Never going to live close to you again –
Cannot look forward to seeing you each week –
That what was going to be, has already been ...
Out time together has too soon passed its peak.
And now – since there're no set times ahead –
No scheduled, wonderful, marvelous things to do –
No way to keep our lives the same – Instead,
I must adjust to a life without you
And all that has meant so very much to me –
When I awoke, the tears fell from my eyes ...
From now on, all I'll have are memories –
And there are no more rainbows in my skies.

Uncertainty

When I try
To look ahead,
I see a wall
Of cold; and dread
To look in back
Of it.

For I cry,
When I look down
And see my feet
Upon the ground –
But feel the lack
Of it.

To Find a Way

I've offered all I have to offer,
Given all I have to give –
If all my efforts do not matter ...
I must find a new way to live.

I have been for you all I can be,
Shown you all I have to show –
If you feel that does not matter ...
I must find a way to go.

I have told you all my feelings,
Shared with you all I can share –
If all my gifts still do not matter ...
I must find my way elsewhere.

If you don't care whether I'm with you,
Do not call me on the phone –
Make me feel I do not matter ...
I must find my way alone.

I have sorrow, for I love you,
And I know my heart will grieve –
For what is lost will always matter ...
I must find a way to leave.

Loving, giving, caring, sharing,
And a heart that won't pretend –
All the things that really matter ...
I must find a way to end.

I will keep my love forever,
Packed away and on a shelf,
Where no one knows – and it doesn't matter ...
I will find my way myself.

It's a shame, for when it's over,
You may come to value me –
For my gifts may someday matter ...
I'll be on my way, and I'll be free.

You Feel the Way You Feel

Heart, why must you take control?
Can't you let me use my mind
Which tells me that I must not love
And must not care and must not feel;
Must you rule my very soul?

Heart, why can't you be content
To hold your love but not to give?
You always trust before you know,
And end still loyal, yet alone;
Can't you ever once relent?

Heart, why must you run my life?
Can't you be like other hearts;
Ruled by reason, disciplined,
Independent, self-controlled;
Must you always cause my strife?

Heart, why won't you ever learn?
Don't you know love causes pain?
Don't you know you will be hurt?
Can't you ever be discreet?
Won't you show some unconcern?

Heart, why must you still defend
Love for love's sake, your crusade?
Must you teach me to believe
That to be loved is not the goal;
To love is in itself an end?

Heart, my heart, oh please be still;
I must not start to love again;
My reason tells me to hold fast,
To stifle feelings – but I know
I cannot change the way I feel.

Heart, I know you'll win again;
I will love and trust and hope;
Giving all I have to give,
Never asking for return;
Loving, yet expecting pain.

We Used to Be

I love the way we used to be
When love had just begun ...
When you and I became a we,
And two turned into one.

When did the we begin to fade,
When did we draw apart?
Why is there now inside of me
A missing piece of heart?

When I Opened My Eyes

I saw you last night!
You came to me
In a dream that was meant
To comfort me ...
You let me know
It was your time to go,
And that you had sent
A sign to me ...

When I opened my eyes,
I knew what I'd find:
The bright shiny dime
You had left behind ...
To let me know
You would always be
Inside my heart
And part of me ...

Review Requested:
If you loved this book, would you please provide a review at Amazon.com?
Thank You

CPSIA information can be obtained
at www.ICGtesting.com
Printed in the USA
LVHW042140160919
631220LV00003B/468

9 781949 483208